MAY EACH NEW DAY FIND YOU FEELING BETTER

WANDA E. BRUNSTETTER

During this time of illness,
may you draw even closer to God
in the days ahead.
You are special,
and He cares for you.
My thoughts and prayers
are with you.

1

THOUGHTS

I'M THINKING OF YOU. . .

Thoughts to make you feel better
Are being sent your way,
Believing God will heal you more
With each passing day.
Remember as you think of Him,
He's always by your side;
No matter what the circumstances,
In Him you can abide.

God is thinking of you today.
Keep your thoughts on Him,
remembering how truly great He is.

The LORD of hosts hath sworn,
saying, Surely as I have thought,
so shall it come to pass;
and as I have purposed,
so shall it stand.

ISAIAH 14:24

How precious also are thy thoughts
unto me, O God!
how great is the sum of them!

PSALM 139:17

A Reminder

Remind yourself today that someone
is thinking of you.
I am. . .God is.
May the Lord speed your healing
as you reflect upon His thoughts, His love,
and His Word.

*For your heavenly Father knoweth that ye
have need of all these things.*

Matthew 6:32

MOMENT
BY MOMENT

Never a trial that He is not there,
Never a burden that He doth not hear,
Never a sorrow that He doth not share,
Moment by moment, I'm under His care.
Never a weakness that He doth not feel,
Never a sickness that He cannot heal,
Moment by moment, in woe or in weal,
Jesus, my Savior, abides with me still.

DANIEL W. WHITTLE, 1893

2

PRAYERS

I'M PRAYING FOR YOU...

Prayers are so helpful when we're hurt or ill,
Asking for God's healing and His precious will.
Pray without ceasing—the Bible tells us to—
God knows about your illness and everything you do.
Keep on praying and believing, thanking as you go;
Remember, God always cares, and He loves you so!

N ever quit praying,
for there is power in prayer.
I'm praying for you today.
May you feel God's touch because of prayer.
May you sense His presence and feel His peace.

Prayer also shall be made for him continually;
and daily shall he be praised.

PSALM 72:15

Each time you pray
your faith will be strengthened.
Each time you pray
know that God hears.

And the prayer of faith
shall save the sick,
and the Lord shall raise him up.

JAMES 5:15

Remember that prayer is nothing more
than making your requests known to God.
Share your pain and sickness with Him,
for He does care!
Just as a flower reaches for the sun,
my prayer is that you will
reach out to God and let His Son
bathe your soul with healing.

SWEET HOUR
OF PRAYER

Sweet hour of prayer, sweet hour of prayer,
That calls me from a world of care,
And bids me at my Father's throne,
Make all my wants and wishes known!

In seasons of distress and grief,
My soul has often found relief,
And oft escaped the tempter's snare,
By thy return, sweet hour of prayer.

WILLIAM W. WALFORD, 1845

3

MEDICINE

THE BEST MEDICINE OF ALL. . .

There are many types of medicine
To help make us well,
Prescriptions from the doctor,
Herbs nutrition centers sell.
God has a special medicine
Which heals from the start.
He tells us in the Bible
To have a merry heart!

G od's special medicine. . .
Rx: Take every day for best effect.

Pleasant words are as an honeycomb,
sweet to the soul,
and health to the bones.

PROVERBS 16:24

A merry heart doeth good like a medicine:
but a broken spirit drieth the bones.

PROVERBS 17:22

THERE IS STRENGTH FOUND IN JOY.

H itherto have ye asked nothing in my name:
ask, and ye shall receive,
that your joy may be full.

JOHN 16:24

For this day is holy unto our LORD:
neither be ye sorry;
for the joy of the LORD is your strength.

NEHEMIAH 8:10

HAPPY THINGS TO THINK ABOUT. . .

Family and friends
Christmas trees
Birthday parties
Cuddling a baby
Chirping birds
A colorful rainbow
Beautiful sunsets
Puppies and kittens
Children playing
Your favorite foods

GOD. . .

He loves you more than anything!

HAPPY THINGS TO DO...

Sing or whistle a tune.
Read a good book.
Enjoy a bubble bath.
Listen to joyful music.
Call a friend on the phone.
Look through old family photos.
Work on a puzzle.
Color or paint a picture.
Watch the birds in your yard.
Study the petals of a flower.

SMILE...

It's free and only uses a few muscles!

THERE IS A BALM IN GILEAD

S ometimes I feel discouraged
And think my work's in vain,
But then the Holy Spirit
Revives my soul again.
There is a balm in Gilead
To make the wounded whole;
There is a balm in Gilead
To heal the sin-sick soul.

AFRO-AMERICAN SPIRITUAL

4

COMFORT

I WISH YOU COMFORT. . .

May you feel God's hand of comfort today.
Look to Him as you pray.
May He give you strength and good health, too.
Bask in His presence; your soul He'll renew.

GOD OFFERS COMFORT TO ALL.

REACH OUT AND TAKE HIS HAND.

B lessed be God,
even the Father of our Lord Jesus Christ,
the Father of mercies,
and the God of all comfort.

2 CORINTHIANS 1:3

JESUS STANDS,

WAITING TO COMFORT YOU NOW.

A nd Jesus stood still,
and commanded him to be called.
And they call the blind man,
saying unto him, Be of good comfort, rise;
he calleth thee.

MARK 10:49

TAKE COMFORT FROM OTHERS. . .

W hen others offer comfort
in your time of need,
Accept their gift of kindness,
In every word and deed.

Wherefore comfort one another
with these words.

1 THESSALONIANS 4:18

TAKE COMFORT FROM GOD. . .

T ake comfort in knowing God cares for you.
He knew you even before you were born.
He feels your pain and wants you to
find comfort in Him.

And now, saith the LORD
that formed me from the womb
to be his servant. . .

ISAIAH 49:5

TURN YOUR EYES UPON JESUS

O soul, are you weary and troubled?
No light in the darkness you see?
There's light from a look at the Savior,
And life more abundant and free!

Turn your eyes upon Jesus;
Look full in His wonderful face,
And the things of earth will grow strangely dim
In the light of His glory and grace.

HELEN H. LEMMEL, 1922

5

TRUST

TRUST GOD IN ALL THINGS. . .

While you are sick,
Praying to get well,
Put your trust in God;
He's the one you should tell.
When you are ill
And feeling a bit down,
Answers for your healing
Are waiting to be found.

GOD WANTS YOU TO TRUST HIM.

He that dwelleth in the secret place
of the most High
shall abide under the shadow of the Almighty.
I will say of the LORD, He is my refuge
and my fortress: my God;
in him will I trust.

PSALM 91:1–2

N othing could be better
than trusting God.
Even in sickness,
God is your fortress;
put your trust in Him.

I t is better to trust in the LORD
than to put confidence in men.

PSALM 118:8

The LORD is good, a strong hold in the day of trouble;
and he knoweth them that trust in him.

NAHUM 1:7

TRUST AND OBEY

Not a shadow can rise,
Not a cloud in the skies,
But His smile quickly drives it away.
Not a doubt nor a fear,
Not a sigh nor a tear,
Can abide while we trust and obey.
Trust and obey, for there's no other way
To be happy in Jesus
Than to trust and obey.

JOHN H. SAMMIS, 1887

6

FAITH

FAITH CAN MOVE MOUNTAINS. . .

F aith is believing
what God says He will do.
He loves you so much;
His promises are true.
Ask Him for healing,
And faith to believe.
God is with you,
He will never leave.

FAITH IS BELIEVING IN THE UNSEEN.

But Jesus turned him about,
and when he saw her, he said,
"Daughter, be of good comfort;
thy faith hath made thee whole."

MATTHEW 9:22

*"The things which are impossible with men
are possible with God."*

LUKE 18:27

EXERCISE YOUR FAITH.

Just like muscles in the body,
we must exercise our faith.
Help your faith move higher by praying often.
Help your faith grow stronger by reading God's Word.
Help your faith be renewed by claiming His promises.
Know that He chooses to heal in many different ways.
Thank Him for healing you in whatever manner He sees best.

FAITH IS
THE VICTORY

To him that overcomes the foe
White raiment shall be given,
Before the angels he shall know
His name confessed in heaven.

Then onwards from the hills of light,
Our hearts with love aflame,
We'll vanquish all the hosts of night
In Jesus' conquering name.

Faith is the victory! Faith is the victory!
O glorious victory that overcomes the world!

JOHN H. YATES, 1891

7

MEDITATION

TO MEDITATE MEANS TO
TAKE TIME OUT FOR REFLECTION. . .

Meditation, or quiet time,
Spent alone with the Lord
Gives you more understanding,
Which should never be ignored.
So while you are recovering,
Meditate upon God's Word.
Remember while you're reading,
It's His voice you have heard.

DRAW CLOSER TO GOD THROUGH MEDITATION.

I will meditate in thy precepts,
and have respect unto thy ways.
I will delight myself in thy statutes:
I will not forget thy word.

PSALM 119:15–16

M editate on God's words
and feel His presence
as you gain strength
and renewal through Him.

And when he had sent the multitudes away,
he went up into a mountain apart to pray:
and when the evening was come,
he was there alone.

MATTHEW 14:23

BE STILL MY SOUL

Be still, my soul; thy God doth undertake
To guide the future as He has the past.
Thy hope, thy confidence let nothing shake,
All now mysterious shall be bright at last.
Be still, my soul; the waves and wind still know
His voice who ruled them while He dwelt below.

KATHARINA VON SCHLEGEL, 1752

8

PEACE

EVERYONE NEEDS PEACE OF MIND. . .

Peace of mind is sometimes hard,
Especially when you're ill.
You worry, fret, and wonder
If you'll ever get well.
Peace of mind is available,
When you look to the Lord;
He fills your heart with peace,
Only His touch can afford.

PEACE CAN BE FOUND
IN GOD'S WORD.

Be careful for nothing;
but in every thing by prayer and supplication
with thanksgiving let your requests
be made known unto God.
And the peace of God,
which passeth all understanding,
shall keep your hearts and minds
through Christ Jesus.

PHILIPPIANS 4:6–7

HIDDEN PEACE

I cannot tell thee whence it came,
   This peace within my breast;
But this I know—there fills my soul
   A strange and tranquil rest.

There's a deep, settled peace in my soul.
There's a deep, settled peace in my soul.
Tho' the billows of sin near me roll,
   He abides, Christ abides.

JOHN S. BROWN, 1899

May you feel a sense of peace that
only God can give.
Look to Him for renewed
health and strength.

Peace I leave with you,
my peace I give unto you:
not as the world giveth, give I unto you.
Let not your heart be troubled,
neither let it be afraid.

JOHN 14:27